FIVE-STAR SOLOS

9 Colorful Piano Solos

DENNIS ALEXANDER

Choosing just the right piece for each student is one of the most important attributes of a good teacher. I love it when I hear things like, "Mr. A., can I please play the piece that Brenda played on the last recital?" or, "Mr. A., the piece that John played is one of the coolest pieces I've ever heard! Do you think I could play it?"

The books in the *Five-Star Solos* series provide students and teachers with a wide variety of pieces at graded levels. An array of styles, colors, tempos, and moods are included in each book. Ballads, waltzes, Latin pieces, contemporary sounds, and "showstoppers" all combine to make teaching fun and exciting. At the same time, students will be rewarded with music that sets them apart from the crowd! Have fun exploring page after page of music that will have students smiling and parents glowing. I hope that you find many new "favorites" in this series, and I wish you continued success and joy in your musical journey!

Dennis Alexander

Dedicated to my friend and colleague Kathleen Theisen—Soprano, Pianist, Conductor, and Music Technology Guru!

Alfred Music
P.O. Box 10003
Van Nuys, CA 91410-0003
alfred.com

ISBN-10: 1-4706-3189-X
ISBN-13: 978-1-4706-3189-5

Cover Photos
Piano keys: © Shutterstock.com / nav • Gold star: © Shutterstock.com / Yulia Glam

LITTLE PRELUDE IN C MAJOR

Dennis Alexander

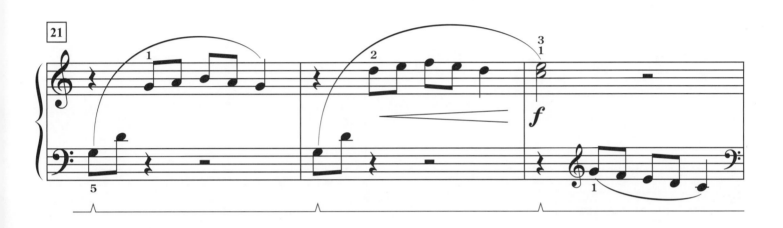

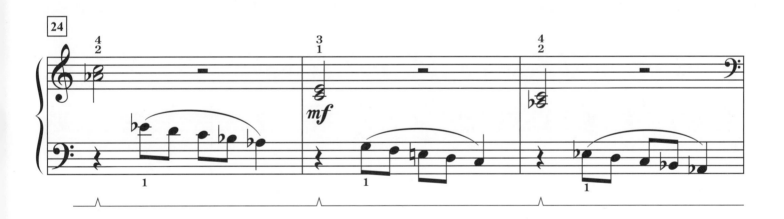

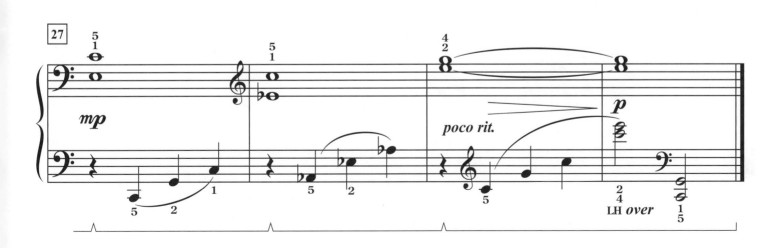

KICK IT ON HOME!

Dennis Alexander

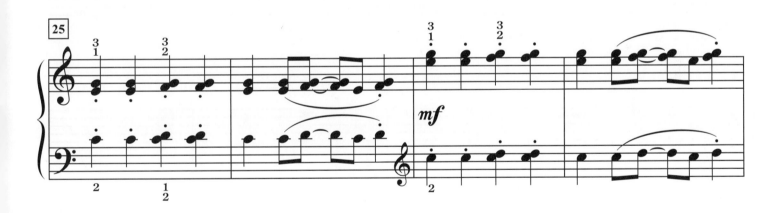

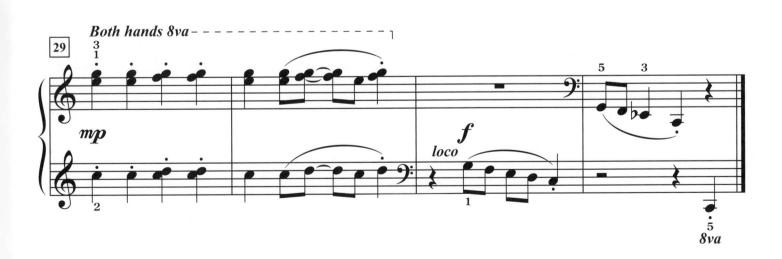

Around Twilight

Dennis Alexander

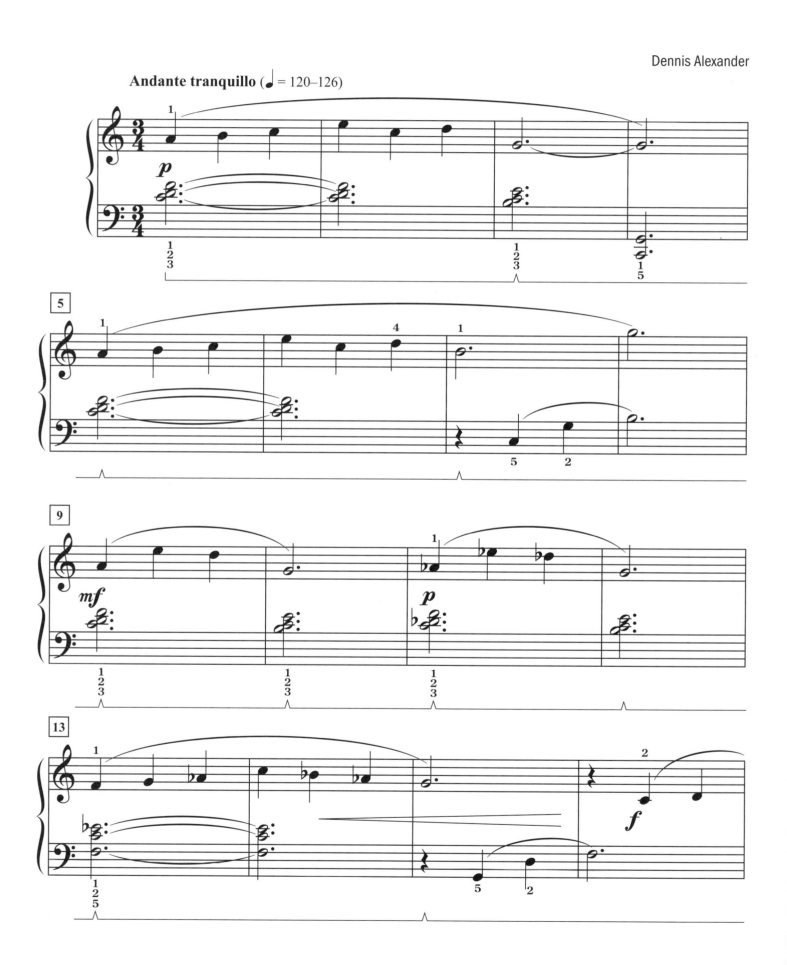

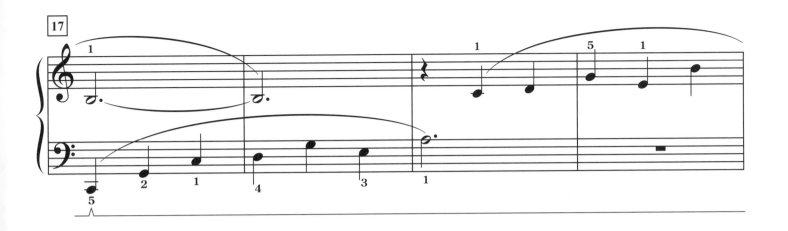

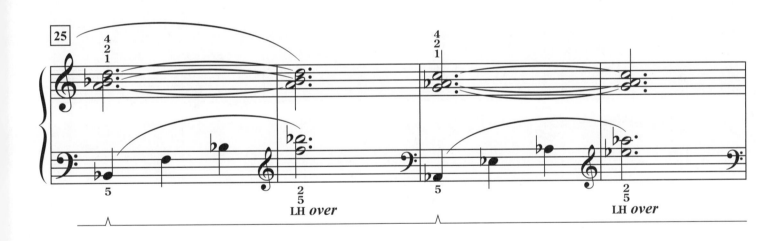

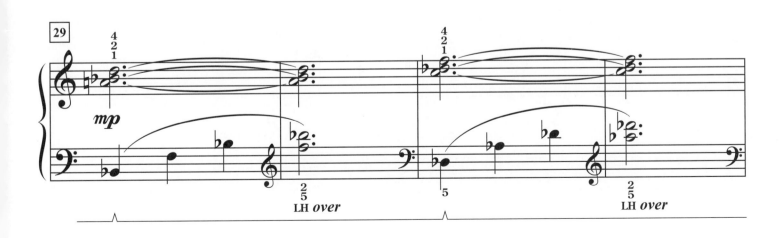

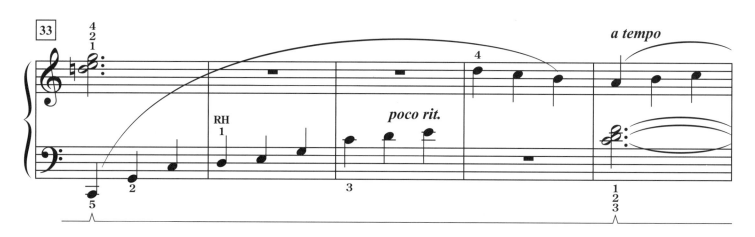

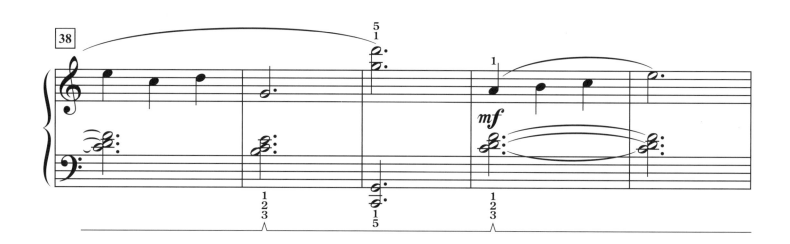

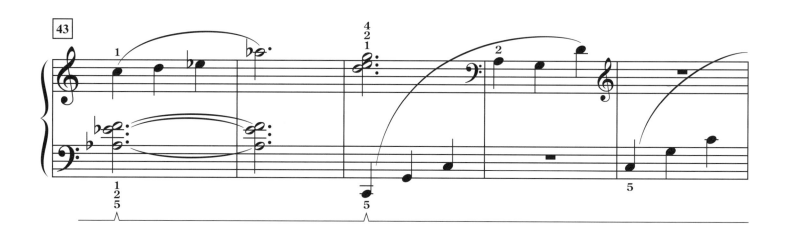

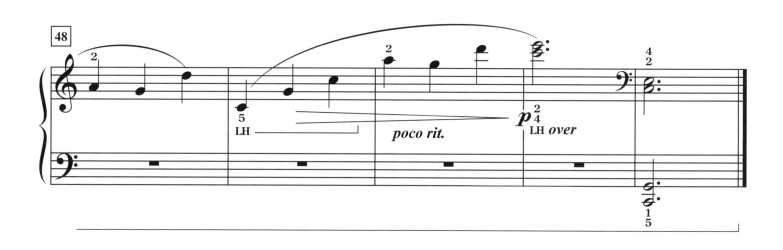

Tarantella Veloce

Dennis Alexander

Scherzino

Dennis Alexander

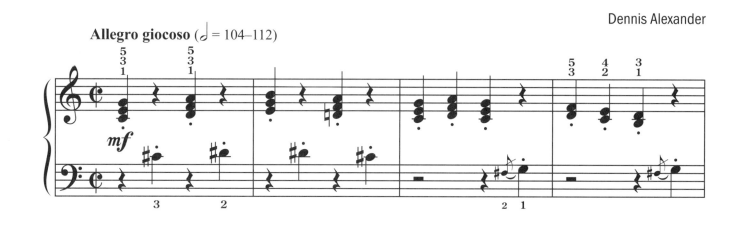

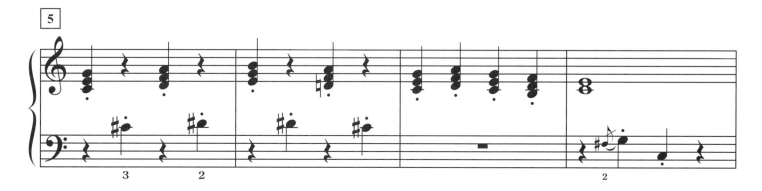

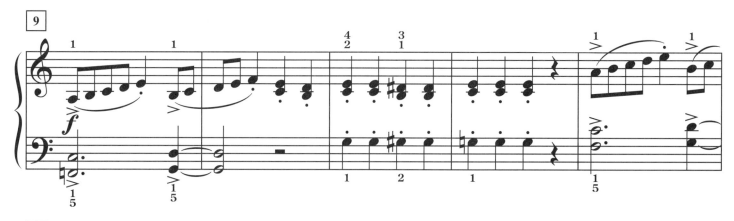

VALSE NOUVEAU

Dennis Alexander

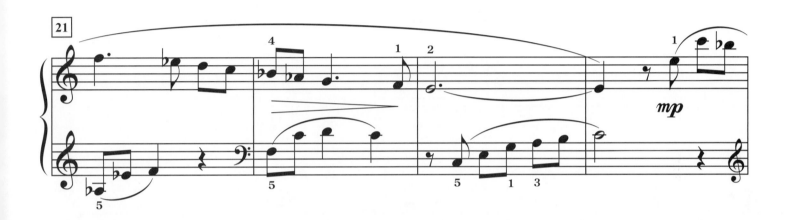

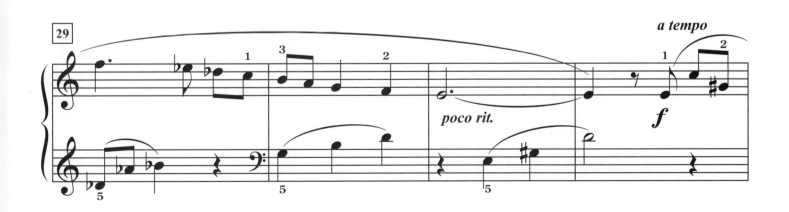

EVER EVOLVING

Dennis Alexander

18

Fleeting Thoughts

Allegretto sciolto (♩ = 63–69)

Dennis Alexander

In the Groove!

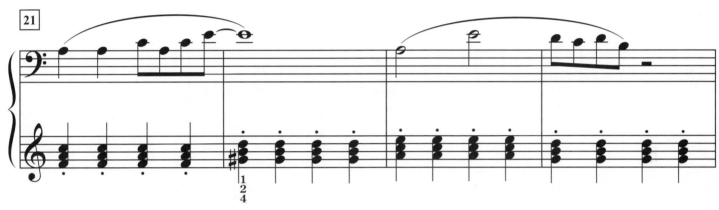

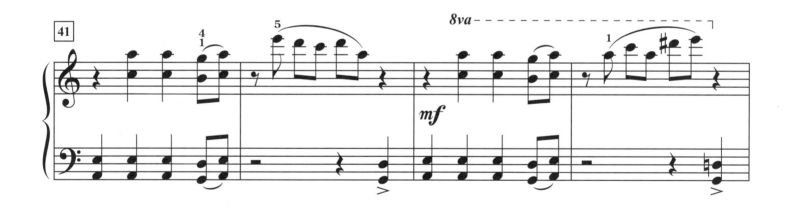

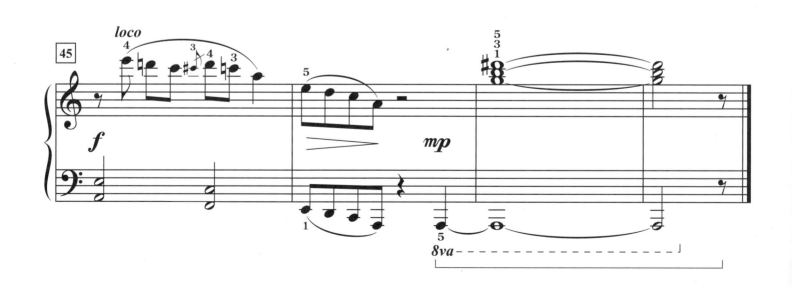